I0017579

Becoming an Influencer on TikTok

The Ultimate Guide

Maxime Luca

ISBN : 9798341325500

Publication Date: October 2024

Table of Contents

Introduction

Introduction to the World of TikTok Influencers

In the vast realm of social media, TikTok has quickly risen as a shining star, drawing in millions of users from around the world. This short-video sharing platform has captured the imagination of people with its playful format, boundless creativity, and its ability to transform ordinary individuals into influential figures. If you are holding this book in your hands, it's because you too have been drawn to the incredible potential TikTok offers for bringing your influencer dreams to life.

But what exactly is an influencer, and how does TikTok stand out from other social networks in this regard? To answer these questions, let's begin by exploring what it truly means to be an influencer in today's social media age. An influencer, in the context of TikTok, is someone who has successfully created a significant and impactful presence on the platform by sharing content that resonates with a devoted audience. This content can take many forms, whether it's dance choreography, makeup tutorials, comedic sketches, musical performances, or even educational videos. A TikTok influencer is someone who knows how to capture viewers' attention in just a few seconds, entertain them, inform them, or even move them emotionally. The world of TikTok influencers is a constantly evolving ecosystem where creativity reigns supreme.

Every day, new talents emerge, and viral videos can catapult unknowns to instant celebrity status. It's a world where music, dance, cinema, and comedy intertwine to create a continuous spectacle that never fails to surprise and captivate a global audience. TikTok has distinguished itself through its powerful recommendation algorithm, which allows users to discover content relevant to them, even if they don't yet follow the influencer in question.

This ability to reach new people has made TikTok particularly attractive to those looking to build an audience from scratch. In this book, we'll dive into the world of TikTok influencers and guide you through the necessary steps to join their ranks. We will explore content creation strategies, audience growth methods, monetization opportunities, and much more. Our goal is to provide you with all the tools you need to succeed on TikTok, whether you want to become a source of inspiration, an entertainment creator, or an expert in your field. So, get ready to dive into this fascinating world, where creativity is king, opportunities are limitless, and you have the potential to become a true force of influence on TikTok. Welcome to the world of TikTok influencers.

The Importance of TikTok in the Social Media Landscape

In recent years, TikTok has emerged as a true revolution in the world of social media. This platform has disrupted established norms and quickly secured a prominent place in the online media landscape. But why has TikTok become so important, and how does it stand out from other social platforms?

1. **Short-Form Content**: TikTok introduced a radically different approach by emphasizing short videos of 15 to 60 seconds. This limited duration forces users to create concise, impactful, and quickly consumable content. In a world where attention spans are increasingly short, TikTok has captured the audience with a format suited to our times.

2. **Democratization of Creativity**: TikTok has broken down the traditional barriers of content creation. You don't need to be a professional actor or a famous musician to

succeed on TikTok. Everyone has the opportunity to become a creator and attract attention through an innovative idea or an authentic performance.

3. **Recommendation Algorithm**: TikTok's algorithm is one of the most powerful and precise among social media platforms. It analyzes user preferences, attention span, interactions, and then proposes a personalized content feed. This allows TikTok to hold its users' attention by showing them content that truly interests them.

4. **Trend Creation**: TikTok has become a generator of cultural trends, whether it's viral dances, memes, popular songs, or challenges. Users actively participate in the creation of these trends, reinforcing a sense of belonging to a global community.

5. **Diverse Audience**: TikTok has users of all ages, but it is particularly popular among younger generations. This age diversity means TikTok can reach a wide range of audiences, making it an attractive platform for influencers and brands.

6. **Monetization Opportunities**: TikTok has introduced several monetization options for

creators, including brand partnerships, virtual gifts, and ads. This has opened up new revenue streams for influencers.

7. **Cultural Impact**: TikTok has played a major role in shaping popular culture, propelling songs to the top of the music charts, creating internet memes, and giving a voice to important social issues. In short, TikTok has brought a new dynamic to social media by emphasizing creativity, authenticity, and fast content consumption. Its influence on the social media landscape cannot be underestimated, and it continues to evolve and shape the way we interact with online media. For aspiring influencers, understanding this significance and mastering TikTok can represent an incredible opportunity to build their online presence.

Who This Book Is For and What You Can Expect

This book is specially designed to meet the needs of anyone eager to embark on the exciting journey of becoming an influencer on TikTok. Whether you're a complete beginner or have some experience on the platform, this guide is tailored to help you achieve your goals and shine as a TikTok influencer. Here's who this book is particularly useful for:

1. **TikTok Beginners**: If you've just created your TikTok account and don't know where to start, this book will provide you with a comprehensive guide to understanding the platform, creating quality content, and growing your audience.

2. **Aspiring Creators**: If you already have a TikTok account but want to improve your presence and expand your influence, this guide will offer advanced tips to optimize your profile, increase your followers, and monetize your content.

3. **Aspiring Influencers**: If your goal is to become a recognized influencer on TikTok, this book will guide you through the necessary steps to build a strong personal brand, collaborate with brands, and make money from your influence.

4. **TikTok Culture Enthusiasts**: Even if you don't intend to become an influencer, this book will give you an in-depth look into TikTok culture, its importance in social media, and its impact on modern pop culture. So, what can you expect from reading this book?

- **A Complete Understanding of TikTok**: You will gain an in-depth knowledge of TikTok, its history, how it works, and its potential as an influencer platform.

- **Practical Tips**: You will discover actionable advice and proven strategies for creating quality content, growing your audience, and managing your presence on TikTok.

- **Inspiring Case Studies**: You will find case studies of successful TikTok influencers, showing how they achieved success and what you can learn from them.

- **Valuable Resources**: Additional resources, tools, and tips on the latest TikTok trends and updates will be provided to keep you up-to-date in an ever-changing environment.

- **Motivation and Inspiration**: You'll be inspired by stories of creators who succeeded on TikTok, encouraging you to pursue your influencer dreams.

- **The Ability to Succeed on TikTok**: Ultimately, this book aims to give you the knowledge and skills needed to excel on TikTok, whether as a passionate content creator, a professional influencer, or just a curious enthusiast.

In short, this book is an essential companion for anyone looking to explore the exciting world of social media and influence on TikTok. It offers a balanced mix of information, inspiration, and practical advice to help you achieve your goals on this dynamic platform.

Chapter 1
Understanding TikTok

A Brief History of TikTok

TikTok has taken the social media world by storm, but understanding its meteoric rise requires going back in time to grasp its origins and rapid evolution.

The Origins of TikTok:

TikTok was born in China under the name "Douyin" in September 2016. Created by the Chinese company ByteDance, its primary goal was to allow users to create and share short musical videos. The app quickly gained massive popularity in China, attracting millions of users in a short time.

The Merger with Musical.ly:

In 2017, ByteDance made a strategic move by acquiring the app Musical.ly, which was already popular outside of China, especially in the U.S. and Europe. By merging Musical.ly with Douyin, ByteDance created what we now know as TikTok. This merger allowed TikTok to become a global platform, combining Douyin's creativity with Musical.ly's international user base.

Global Expansion:

TikTok launched internationally in 2018, marking the start of its global dominance. Users worldwide quickly adopted the app to share a variety of content, from dance and comedy to educational and informative videos. TikTok became a cultural phenomenon and a social media powerhouse.

TikTok's Algorithm:

One of the key elements behind TikTok's rapid growth is its recommendation algorithm. Unlike other platforms that rely on subscriptions, TikTok uses a powerful algorithm that quickly identifies user preferences. It analyzes data such as likes, shares, and watch time to suggest relevant content to each user. This has created massive engagement, encouraging people to spend more and more time on the platform.

The Culture of Challenges and Trends:

TikTok has also thrived on its culture of viral challenges and trends. Users actively create and participate in viral challenges, choreographies, memes, and other cultural trends. This has contributed to the creation of a dynamic and interactive community.

Role in Pop Culture:

TikTok quickly gained importance in pop culture by propelling songs to the top of the charts, popularizing viral dances, and creating internet celebrities. It has also played a role in spreading political and social messages, reinforcing its relevance beyond pure entertainment.

In summary, TikTok is more than just a video-sharing app. It's a platform that has evolved quickly into a major player in social media, influencing culture and creating new opportunities for content creators worldwide. Understanding TikTok's history and impact is essential for anyone looking to embark on the exciting journey of becoming an influencer or creator on the platform.

Key Statistics and Current Trends

To succeed as an influencer on TikTok, it's essential to understand key statistics and stay updated with current trends. Keeping an eye on these numbers can help you refine your strategy, target your content more effectively, and remain relevant in TikTok's ever-evolving community. Here are some of the most important stats and trends to consider:

1. **User Numbers:**

   TikTok surpassed 2 billion downloads in 2021, making it one of the most popular apps in the world. Users are present in more than 150 countries, with a growing base in the U.S., India, Brazil, and Europe.

2. **Age Demographics:**

   Although TikTok is used by people of all ages, it remains particularly popular among younger audiences. Generation Z and millennials are the most active demographic groups on the platform.

3. **Time Spent on the App:**

TikTok is famous for its ability to hold users' attention. On average, users spend around 52 minutes per day on the app, a significant figure compared to other social platforms.

4. **Engagement:**
   TikTok sees high engagement, with plenty of likes, comments, and shares. Users actively interact with the content they enjoy, creating numerous opportunities for creators.

5. **Viral Content:**

   Viral videos are a defining feature of TikTok. Trends, challenges, and music videos can quickly gain traction and be shared massively.

6. **Influencers:**
   TikTok has seen the rise of many famous influencers who have amassed millions of followers and built strong personal brands. These influencers have played a key role in the platform's popularity.

7. **Monetization:**
   TikTok has introduced monetization options for creators, including brand partnerships, virtual gifts, and ads. Content creators now have the opportunity to generate income through their TikTok presence.

8. **Creative Trends:**

TikTok is constantly evolving, with new creative trends emerging regularly. Creators who stay ahead of these trends can capitalize on their popularity.

9. **Educational Content:**

   TikTok has seen a rise in educational content, including tutorials, tips, and informative videos. This trend offers opportunities for content creators who are experts in their fields.

10. **Social and Political Issues:**

   TikTok has also been a platform for discussions on important social and political issues. Engaging and informative videos are gaining popularity, showing that the platform is used for more than just entertainment.

As a TikTok influencer, it's crucial to keep an eye on these statistics and trends as they can help you tailor your content, engage with your audience more effectively, and seize collaboration opportunities with brands. TikTok remains a constantly evolving platform, and those who adapt to its changes will have the best chance of succeeding in this dynamic space.

Why Is TikTok So Popular?

1. **Short, Captivating Format:**

   One of the key factors behind TikTok's popularity is its short-form videos of 15 to 60 seconds. This format is perfectly suited to the short attention spans of today's world. It allows creators to quickly capture viewers' attention and deliver their message concisely and powerfully.

2. **Unlimited Creativity:**

   TikTok encourages creativity in all its forms. Users can create a wide range of content, from dances and musical performances to comedy sketches, tutorials, recipes, beauty tips, and much more. This variety of content stimulates the imagination of creators and offers something for every passion or interest.

3. **Powerful Recommendation Algorithm:**

   TikTok features a highly sophisticated recommendation algorithm. It analyzes real-time user behavior, such as the videos they like, share, and watch until the end. Using this data, TikTok suggests relevant content, keeping users engaged and encouraging the exploration of new videos.

4. **Ease of Use:**

   TikTok is designed to be user-friendly, even for beginners. The app offers a simple interface and a range of creation, editing, and special effects tools accessible to all. This simplicity allows a wide range of people to become creators on the platform.

5. **Viral Trends and Challenges:**

   TikTok is a hotbed for viral trends and challenges. Users love participating in these trends by creating their own videos, fostering strong interactivity and encouraging content to go viral.

6. **Music at the Core:**

   Music plays a central role on TikTok. Users can add song clips to their videos, which has contributed to the popularity of many tracks. TikTok has also partnered with the music industry, giving it access to a vast musical catalog.

7. **Cultural Diversity:**

   TikTok is an international platform, meaning users from around the world share their culture, language, dances, and traditions. This cultural diversity enriches the user experience and allows TikTok to reach a global audience.

8. **Opportunities for Creativity:**

   TikTok offers a unique opportunity for creators to gain recognition quickly. Many influencers and celebrities have emerged on TikTok in a short time, attracting more and more people seeking a platform to express their creativity.

9. **Pandemic Response:**

TikTok experienced even faster growth during the COVID-19 pandemic. People sought entertainment, connection with others, and creative expression while staying home, which amplified the platform's popularity.

10. **Engaged Community:**

TikTok is more than just a social media platform; it's an engaged community. Users actively interact with content they like, leaving likes, comments, and sharing videos. This creates a sense of belonging and strengthens user engagement.

In conclusion, TikTok has become a global phenomenon due to its ability to captivate attention, encourage creativity, and foster an engaged community. Its short format, intelligent algorithm, and openness to cultural diversity make it a unique platform that continues to redefine how we create and consume content online.

Chapter 2

Account Creation and Settings

Creating a TikTok Account

The first crucial step to becoming an influencer on TikTok is creating an account on the platform. Though this might seem simple, it's fundamental to establishing your presence and starting your content creation journey. Here's a detailed guide to setting up a TikTok account:

1. **Download the App**: Head over to the App Store (for iOS users) or Google Play (for Android users) and download the TikTok app. It's usually free and easy to find by simply searching for "TikTok."

2. **Launching the App**: Once installed, open the app. You'll be greeted by TikTok's welcome screen, where you can view popular videos of the moment, even without an account.

3. **Creating the Account**: To create your TikTok account, tap the "Me" icon at the bottom right of the screen. Then tap "Sign Up" to begin the registration process.

4. **Choosing a Sign-Up Method**: TikTok offers multiple ways to sign up, including using your

phone number, email address, or linking your Facebook or Google account. Choose the method that suits you best. Phone number registration is often the most common.

5. **Identity Verification**: Follow the steps to verify your identity by providing the required information, such as your phone number or email address. You'll also need to create a secure password.

6. **Creating Your Username**: Choose a unique username that represents you on TikTok. Keep in mind that your username can influence the first impression others will have of you.

7. **Privacy Settings**: At this stage, you'll be prompted to set your privacy preferences. You can choose to make your account public, private (which means you'll have to approve followers), or visible only to your friends.

8. **Profile Customization**: Personalize your profile by adding a profile picture, a cover photo, and writing a short bio. Your profile picture is often the first thing people will see, so choose one that reflects your personality or niche.

9. **Linking to Other Accounts**: If you want, you can link your TikTok account to other social

platforms like Instagram or YouTube. This allows users to find you more easily across platforms.

10. **Explore and Follow**: Once your account is set up, explore TikTok by browsing videos and following other users. This will help you get familiar with the platform and discover current trends.

11. **Creating Your First Video**: You're ready to start! Tap the "Plus" icon at the bottom of the screen to create your first video. You can use TikTok's features like music, special effects, and editing tools to make your video stand out.

Creating a TikTok account is an exciting step towards achieving your influencer goals on the platform. Make sure to customize your profile to reflect your style and niche, and don't forget to follow other users to create connections and find inspiring content. Once your account is set up, you're ready to dive into TikTok's creative universe and start sharing your own content with the world.

Profile Setup

After creating your TikTok account, it's time to customize your profile to reflect your identity and style. Your profile is the first impression other users will have of you, so it's important to make it both attractive and informative. Here's how to set up your TikTok profile:

1. **Add a Profile Picture**: Your profile picture is the first thing other users will see when you interact with them on TikTok. Choose a clear, recognizable image of yourself or your brand. A headshot is often recommended as it creates a personal connection with others.

2. **Customize the Cover Photo**: The cover photo is the image that appears at the top of your profile. It can reflect your personality, passion, or niche. Some users prefer to leave this space blank for a clean look, while others add a meaningful image.

3. **Write an Engaging Bio**: The bio is where you can briefly introduce yourself and explain what other users can expect from your account. Keep it short and concise, but make sure it clearly communicates what you

represent on TikTok. You can also add emojis for some personality.

4. **Link Other Accounts**: If you have accounts on other social platforms like Instagram, YouTube, or Twitter, you can link them to your TikTok profile. This allows users to easily find you on these platforms and discover more of your content.

5. **Set Privacy Preferences**: Choose the privacy settings that work best for you. You can make your account public, private (where you must approve followers), or visible only to friends. This decision depends on your goal and how you want to interact with your audience.

6. **Customize Your TikTok URL**: If you meet the eligibility requirements, you can customize your TikTok URL. This will give you an easy-to-remember URL, which is useful if you share your account on other platforms or with friends.

7. **Add Links and Contacts**: You can add links to your website, YouTube channel, or other relevant links. You can also sync your contacts to find friends who are already on TikTok.

8. **Specify Your Interests**: You can select categories of interest that match your tastes and niche. This helps TikTok recommend

relevant content and connect you with other users who share similar interests.

9. **Enable Notifications**: You can customize notifications to receive alerts on interactions with your account, comments, likes, and other activities. This helps you stay connected with your audience.

By carefully setting up your TikTok profile, you create a strong foundation for your presence on the platform. A well-maintained and engaging profile encourages others to follow and interact with you. Keep in mind that your profile can evolve over time to reflect your growth and changes as a TikTok influencer.

Privacy Settings

TikTok's privacy settings are essential for managing your presence on the platform and controlling who can access your content and interact with you. It's important to customize these settings based on your goals as an influencer. Here's a detailed guide to TikTok's privacy settings:

1. **Public, Private, or Friends-Only Account**: You can choose the level of visibility for your account.
   • **Public Account**: If your account is public, anyone can view your videos, follow you, and interact with you without prior approval. This is ideal if you want to reach a larger audience and attract new followers quickly.
   • **Private Account**: If you set your account to private, only people you approve will be able to follow you and view your content. This gives you more control over who can access your profile but can also limit your reach.
   • **Friends-Only**: You can also choose to allow only your TikTok friends to follow and interact with you. This is the most restrictive option in terms of audience, but it ensures

that only approved contacts can see your content.

2. **Follower Approval (Private Account)**: If you have a private account, TikTok allows you to approve or reject follow requests. You can review the profiles of those who want to follow you and decide if they fit your target audience before accepting them.

3. **Direct Messages**: You can control who can send you direct messages. Options include "Everyone," "Friends," or "Disabled." Managing direct messages can be helpful for controlling interactions with your audience.

4. **Comments and Replies**: You can restrict who can comment on your videos and who can reply to your comments. You can choose from "Everyone," "Friends," or "People You Follow." This allows you to filter comments and responses to avoid inappropriate or irrelevant content.

5. **Disabling Comments**: If you prefer not to have comments on certain videos, you can disable comments for those specific videos. This option is useful if you're posting sensitive content or want to avoid unwanted interactions.

6. **Blocking and Reporting**: TikTok offers blocking and reporting features for unwanted users or inappropriate content. You can block specific users to prevent them from following or contacting you, and you can report content that violates TikTok's community guidelines.

7. **Personal Information**: Be careful not to share sensitive personal information in your public profile. This includes details like your address, phone number, and email.

8. **Two-Factor Authentication**: To strengthen your account's security, you can enable two-factor authentication. This adds an extra layer of protection by requiring a one-time security code when you log in to your account.

9. **Custom Notifications**: You can personalize notifications to receive alerts for specific activities, such as likes, new followers, or comments. This keeps you efficiently informed.

By smartly adjusting these privacy settings, you can create a safe environment tailored to your needs on TikTok. Whether you want to reach a broad audience or restrict access to your content, TikTok

offers flexible options to customize your experience
and protect your privacy as an influencer.

Chapter 3

Creating Quality Content

Identifying Your Niche and Audience

Creating quality content on TikTok begins with a deep understanding of your niche and target audience. It's essential to know who you're targeting and what you have to offer in order to succeed as an influencer on the platform. Here's how to identify your niche and audience:

1. **Identifying Your Niche**:

    o **Define Your Passion or Expertise**: Start by reflecting on what you're most passionate about. What are your interests? In which area do you have expertise? Your niche could be related to fashion, cooking, beauty, fitness, travel, comedy, tech, education, or any other field you're passionate about.

    o **Trend Research**: Analyze current trends on TikTok to see if your passion aligns with a popular niche. You can use trend research tools or explore the most popular videos to spot trending topics.

- **Evaluate the Competition**: Check what other creators in your niche are doing. What type of content are they posting? How are they engaging with their audience? This will help you identify opportunities and gaps that you can capitalize on.

- **Define Your Unique Angle**: Even if your niche is popular, find a unique angle that sets you apart from other creators. What makes you special or different? Your unique perspective can be your strength.

2. **Identifying Your Target Audience**:

- **Create an Audience Profile**: Visualize your ideal audience. How old are they? Where do they live? What are their interests? What problems can you solve for them? The more you understand your audience, the easier it will be to create content that resonates with them.

- **Analyze Audience Insights**: Once you've posted a few videos, use TikTok's analytics to learn more about your audience. You can see the average age, gender, and geographical location of your followers, which helps you refine your strategy.

o **Engage with Your Audience**: Interact regularly with your followers by responding to comments and considering their feedback. This strengthens audience loyalty and helps you better understand their needs.

o **Create Content for Your Audience**: Based on what you've learned about your audience, create content that addresses their interests, questions, and concerns. Provide value to your audience to keep them engaged.

Identifying your niche and audience is a crucial step in succeeding on TikTok. Once you have a clear understanding of your niche and audience, you can create content that resonates with them in a meaningful way. Your content will be more relevant, engaging, and likely to attract new followers, which is key to growing your influence on the platform.

The Different Types of TikTok Content (Music, Dance, Sketches, Tutorials, etc.)

TikTok offers a wide variety of content formats, allowing creators to express their creativity and engage with their audience in different ways. One of the most captivating aspects of TikTok is the diversity of content types you can create. Here's an overview of the most popular types of content on the platform:

1. **Musical Videos**: Musical videos are at the core of TikTok. You can choose from a vast library of songs to create videos synced to music. Many trends and challenges on TikTok are centered around music clips.

2. **Dance**: Dance videos are among the most popular on TikTok. Creators invent and share choreography, and other users imitate it by

adding their own style. Viral dances can quickly gain popularity.

3. **Sketches and Comedy**: TikTok is an ideal platform for creating comedic sketches and humorous videos. You can play different roles, tell jokes, or create funny scenarios to entertain your audience.

4. **Tutorials**: Tutorials are highly appreciated on TikTok. You can teach skills, give advice, or share tips in short videos. Tutorials can cover a range of topics, from cooking to beauty to DIY projects.

5. **Education**: TikTok offers a unique platform for education. You can explain complex concepts in simple terms, present interesting facts, or share educational information on various subjects.

6. **Informative Content**: Informative videos cover a wide array of topics, such as science, technology, health, and culture. You can explain phenomena, debunk myths, or raise awareness about important issues.

7. **Recipes and Cooking**: Cooking is a popular topic on TikTok. You can share recipes, cooking tips, or even show how to prepare dishes. Cooking videos are often very visual and appetizing.

8. **Travel**: Travelers can share their adventures, give recommendations for destinations, or show travel tips. TikTok allows you to virtually experience travel.

9. **Challenges and Trends**: TikTok is known for its viral challenges and trends. You can participate in existing challenges or create your own to encourage audience engagement.

10. **Personal Stories**: Some creators share personal stories, testimonies, or life experiences. These videos can be powerful in creating a connection with your audience.

11. **Vlogs**: Vlogs allow you to share your daily life or special events. Vlogs can be informal and offer an authentic glimpse into your personality.

12. **Branded Content**: As an influencer, you can also create content in partnership with brands. This can include product reviews, demonstrations, or recommendations.

The key to succeeding on TikTok is finding the type of content that best matches your personality, skills, and niche. Experiment with different formats to discover what works best for you and your audience. Don't hesitate to combine various content types to keep your TikTok profile engaging and diverse.

Creation Tools: Special Effects, Editing, Music

The creation tools available on TikTok are essential for producing high-quality and captivating content. They allow creators to personalize their videos, add special effects, create creative edits, and integrate music to make their videos more appealing. Here's an overview of the main creation tools available on TikTok:

1. **Special Effects**: TikTok offers a wide range of special effects that can transform your videos dramatically. You can add filters, slow-motion, fast-forward, distortion, blur, mirror effects, colors, and more. These effects allow you to add a unique touch to your videos and grab viewers' attention.

2. **Video Editing**: TikTok has built-in video editing tools that allow you to cut, split, merge, and rearrange video clips. You can also adjust playback speed, add smooth transitions between clips, and use advanced editing features to fine-tune your content.

3. **Music**: TikTok offers a vast music library with thousands of songs from different genres.

You can add music to your videos to create content synced to popular tracks, sound effects, or even movie quotes. The choice of music can significantly influence your video's mood.

4. **Text and Stickers**: You can add custom text to your videos to explain, narrate, or add commentary. Stickers, emojis, and animated stickers are also available to add a playful touch to your videos.

5. **Voice-over**: TikTok's voice-over tool allows you to record a voice commentary to accompany your video. This is useful for explaining something, telling a story, or giving instructions while showing images.

6. **Time-lapse and Slow-motion**: You can adjust the playback speed of your videos to create fast time-lapse effects or dramatic slow-motion. This adds a creative dimension to your videos.

7. **Shooting Functions**: TikTok offers time-lapse shooting functions that allow you to capture a series of short clips and assemble them into one longer video. This function is ideal for travel or transformation videos.

8. **Transition Effects**: You can add smooth transitions between clips to make your video

more professional and engaging. TikTok offers a variety of transition effects, such as fade, swipe, zoom, and more.

9. **Advanced Editing**: TikTok offers advanced editing features, such as adjusting brightness, contrast, saturation, and color. You can also add subtitles, captions, and blur effects for a more customized look.

10. **Cutting Effects**: You can cut out unwanted parts of your videos or add cutting effects to create sharper, more dynamic transitions.

By using these creation tools creatively, you can make your TikTok content more engaging, entertaining, and professional. Combining special effects, music, editing, and storytelling can help capture your audience's attention and bring your ideas to life. Don't hesitate to explore these features to see how they can enhance the quality of your TikTok content.

Strategies for Creating Viral Videos

Creating viral videos on TikTok is the goal of many creators on the platform. However, it requires a deep understanding of TikTok's audience, current trends, and the elements that make a video engaging. Here are some strategies to help you create viral TikTok videos:

1. **Stay on Top of Trends**: Trends emerge quickly on TikTok. Keep an eye on the latest trends by exploring the "Discover" page and regularly checking popular videos. Participating in challenges and trending topics can increase your content's visibility.

2. **Create a Memorable Hook**: The beginning of your video should grab viewers' attention immediately. Use an intriguing hook, a provocative question, or a captivating action within the first few seconds to keep people watching until the end.

3. **Be Creative and Original**: Creativity is essential on TikTok. Find unique ways to present your content. Avoid simply copying

what works for other creators. Original videos are more likely to stand out.

4. **Use Popular Music**: Incorporate popular songs into your videos. Music adds an emotional and memorable dimension to your content. Ensure the music matches the tone of your video.

5. **Leverage Humor**: Humorous videos are widely shared on TikTok. If you have a sense of humor, use it to create funny videos that make your audience laugh and smile.

6. **Keep it Concise**: TikTok videos are short, so every second counts. Avoid long introductions and get straight to the point. Your message or story should be clear and engaging from the beginning.

7. **Use Special Effects**: Special effects can add visual interest to your video. Experiment with filters, transitions, slow-motion, fast-forward effects, and more to create visually appealing content.

8. **Engage with Your Audience**: Interact with comments and direct messages. Respond to questions, thank followers, and be present in the comments section. Active engagement fosters a sense of community and can encourage people to share your content.

9. **Post at Strategic Times**: The timing of your post can impact your video's visibility. Post when your audience is most active. This may vary based on your geographic location and niche.

10. **Use Relevant Hashtags**: Use popular and relevant hashtags for your content. Hashtags help people find your video when they search for specific topics. However, don't overdo it, as it may appear spammy.

11. **Collaborate with Other Creators**: Collaborating with other creators can expand your audience. Working with creators who have a similar follower base can help boost the visibility of your content.

12. **Analyze Your Stats**: Use TikTok's analytics tools to track your video performance. Identify what works and what doesn't, then adjust your strategy accordingly.

13. **Be Consistent**: Consistency is key to building a loyal audience. Regularly post quality content to maintain engagement and grow your follower base.

14. **Learn from Failures**: Don't be discouraged by videos that don't go viral. Learn from the videos that were less successful and use those experiences to improve future content.

Creating viral videos on TikTok can be challenging, but by understanding your audience's preferences, staying creative, and keeping up with trends, you increase your chances of success. Remember, virality is never guaranteed, but quality content and persistence are key to reaching a larger audience.

Chapter 4
Profile
Optimization

Optimizing Your Bio and Profile Picture

Optimizing your TikTok profile is crucial for attracting users and encouraging them to follow your account. Your bio and profile picture are the first elements visitors will see when they land on your profile. Here's how to optimize them effectively:

1. **Profile Picture:** Your profile picture is your first impression on TikTok, so it needs to be chosen carefully. Here are some tips for optimizing your profile picture:

   o **Clarity and Recognizability:** Use a clear and sharp profile picture. Faces are often recommended as they help create a personal connection with users. Make sure your face is well-lit and easily recognizable.

   o **Brand Consistency:** If you're creating content for a brand or business, use the brand's logo as your profile picture to reinforce brand recognition.

- **Avoid Blurry' or Inappropriate Photos:** Avoid blurry, pixelated, or inappropriate photos. A professional profile picture suited to your niche is important for establishing credibility.

- **Regular Updates:** If your appearance changes over time (e.g., hairstyle, style, or brand logo), make sure to update your profile picture to reflect these changes.

2. **Bio:** Your TikTok bio is an opportunity to briefly introduce your account and give visitors a sense of what they can expect from your content. Here's how to optimize your bio:

   - **Be Concise:** Your bio has limited space, so be concise. Clearly communicate your niche or passion in a few sentences. You can also add emojis to showcase your personality.

   - **Use Relevant Keywords:** If possible, include relevant keywords related to your niche or content. This can help your profile appear in relevant search results.

   - **Call to Action:** Encourage visitors to follow your account or check out your latest content by using a call to action. For example, you could write: "Follow for weekly beauty tips" or "Check out my delicious recipes here!"

- o **Links and Contacts:** If you have other social media accounts or a website, add links in your bio to direct users to those platforms. You can also sync your contacts to find friends on TikTok.

- o **Show Your Personality:** Let your personality shine through in your bio. Whether you're funny, serious, or passionate, ensure that your bio reflects your style and tone.

- o **Frequent Updates:** If you have important announcements or updates, feel free to add them to your bio. This could include special events, upcoming collaborations, or new content.

Optimizing your profile picture and bio is an essential aspect of building an effective TikTok presence. These elements contribute to your account's credibility, personality, and clarity. When visitors land on your profile, they should immediately understand what you offer and be encouraged to engage with your content. Take the time to fine-tune these details to maximize the impact of your TikTok profile.

Using Hashtags

Using hashtags effectively on TikTok can significantly increase the visibility of your content, attract new followers, and contribute to the virality of your videos. Here's how to use hashtags strategically on TikTok:

1. **Understand the Importance of Hashtags:** Hashtags are essential on TikTok because they help categorize content and allow users to discover videos on topics they're interested in. By using the right hashtags, you increase your chances of appearing in search results and on the "Discover" pages.

2. **Research Relevant Hashtags:** Before choosing hashtags, do some research to find those relevant to your niche or specific content. Use TikTok's search function to discover popular hashtags related to your topic.

3. **Be Specific:** Use specific hashtags that accurately describe the content of your video. For example, if you're posting a chocolate cake recipe, use hashtags like #ChocolateCakeRecipe or #Baking.

4. **Mix Popular and Less Popular Hashtags:** It's smart to use a combination of both popular and less popular hashtags. Popular hashtags can give you greater visibility, but competition can be tough. Less popular hashtags can help you stand out and reach a more targeted audience.

5. **Avoid Hashtag Overload:** Although TikTok allows up to 100 characters in the video description, it's better to avoid using too many hashtags. Three to five relevant hashtags are usually enough. Using too many can seem spammy.

6. **Use Challenge and Trend Hashtags:** If you're participating in a popular TikTok challenge or trend, be sure to include the associated hashtag. This will help you appear in that challenge or trend's gallery, attracting attention from a broader audience.

7. **Create Your Own Hashtag:** If you have a niche or specific video series, consider creating your own custom hashtag. This can encourage others to join your community and generate content related to your niche.

8. **Monitor Hashtag Performance:** Use TikTok's analytics tools to track how well your videos are performing with specific hashtags. This

allows you to see which hashtags bring the most engagement and followers.

9. **Be Creative with Hashtags:** Hashtags don't have to be boring. You can incorporate them creatively into your video, such as during transitions, writing them on a board, or using them as part of the narrative.

10. **Stay Updated with Trends:** Hashtag trends change quickly on TikTok. Make sure to keep up with current trends and adjust your hashtags accordingly to stay relevant.

Using hashtags wisely can be a major asset for your visibility and the growth of your TikTok account. When you choose and use hashtags strategically, you increase your chances of reaching a wider audience and sparking interest from new followers. However, ensure the hashtags you select are relevant to your content to attract an authentic and engaged audience.

Interacting with Other Users

Interacting with other users on TikTok is a key aspect of growing your presence on the platform and increasing your follower base. Here's how to effectively engage with other users on TikTok:

1. **Respond to Comments:** When users comment on your videos, take the time to reply. Responding to comments shows that you are engaged with your audience and value their feedback. This can encourage more comments and participation.

2. **Follow and Interact with Other Creators:** Follow accounts that share similar or complementary interests to yours. Engage with their content by liking, commenting, and sharing. This interaction can attract their attention and encourage them to visit your profile.

3. **Participate in Challenges and Trends:** Actively participating in popular TikTok challenges and trends increases your chances of attracting other users' attention who are engaging in the same challenges.

Use the associated hashtags and add your own creativity to stand out.

4. **Collaborate with Other Creators:** Collaborating with other creators is a great way to broaden your audience. Find creators whose content complements yours and propose collaborations. This could include duets, joint videos, or participating in challenges together.

5. **Create Reaction Videos:** You can create reaction videos in response to other users' videos. This means reacting to their content by commenting on or highlighting it. It's a way to show appreciation for their work and interact with their audience.

6. **Share Others' Content:** If you come across interesting content created by other users, share it on your own profile. Be sure to give credit to the original creator by tagging them in the description or using proper sharing tools.

7. **Use TikTok Live:** TikTok Live offers a unique opportunity to interact with your audience in real-time. During a live session, you can answer questions, chat with viewers, and build a direct connection with them.

8. **Host Q&A Sessions:** Q&A sessions are a great way to interact with your audience by answering their questions. You can announce a Q&A session in advance and encourage followers to ask questions in the comments.

9. **Encourage Engagement:** In your videos, actively encourage viewers to engage with your content. Ask questions, request feedback, or propose challenges to encourage comments, likes, and shares.

10. **Stay Respectful and Positive:** When interacting with other users, maintain a respectful and positive tone, even in cases of disagreement. Online respect is essential to maintaining a healthy and enjoyable community.

Engaging with other users on TikTok not only increases your visibility but also helps create genuine connections with your audience and build an engaged community around your content. The more you invest in interacting with users, the more your TikTok presence can thrive. Authenticity and sincerity in your interactions are key factors in building a loyal and engaged follower base.

Collaborations and Duets

Collaborations and duets on TikTok are an excellent way to expand your audience, create authentic interactions with other creators, and produce innovative content. Here's how to approach collaborations and duets effectively on TikTok:

Collaborations:

1. **Identify Relevant Creators**: Look for creators whose content complements yours. For example, if you are a fashion creator, collaborate with other fashion or beauty creators. Make sure the collaboration makes sense for your niche and audience.

2. **Reach Out**: Once you've identified creators you'd like to collaborate with, reach out. Send a direct message to discuss the idea of collaboration and how you can work together.

3. **Define the Concept**: Discuss the concept of the collaboration video. It's important that both parties have a clear understanding of

what they will create. Ensure the concept is interesting and engaging for your audience.

4. **Plan the Production**: Organize the production of the video in collaboration. This may involve preliminary meetings, joint recording sessions, or sharing resources to create the content. Make sure everything is ready for the agreed-upon publishing date.

5. **Give Credit**: When the collaboration video is posted, ensure you give proper credit to the other creator. Mention their name in the video description and tag them in the video if possible.

Duets:

1. **Choose a Creator for a Duet**: For a duet, you can choose an existing video from another creator and make your own version. Look for videos that inspire you or that make you want to create a response or replication.

2. **Record Your Part**: Record your part of the duet using the original video as a reference. Make sure to match the rhythm, movements, and words of the original video if necessary.

3. **Upload the Video**: Once your part is recorded, upload it to TikTok using the "Duet" option during the upload process. This will

automatically pair your video with the original creator's.

4. **Mention the Original Creator**: In the description of your video, mention the original creator by using their username. This will allow viewers to discover the original video.

Important Tips:

- **Communicate Clearly**: Communication is essential during collaborations and duets. Make sure all details are discussed and understood before starting production.

- **Respect Copyright**: When using another creator's video for a duet, ensure you respect copyright by properly giving credit.

- **Ensure the Collaboration Makes Sense**: Collaborations should make sense for your content and audience. Avoid collaborating just for the exposure—ensure that the collaboration adds value to your followers.

- **Promote the Collaboration**: After the collaboration or duet video is posted, be sure to promote it on your social media and mention the other creator to boost visibility.

Collaborations and duets are a fantastic way to diversify your content, build connections with other creators, and attract a wider audience. They also allow you to inject creativity into your content by leveraging the ideas and styles of different creators. When well-planned and executed, collaborations can be a win-win strategy for all participants.

Chapter 5

Audience Growth

Organic Growth Strategies

Growing your TikTok audience organically requires consistent effort and a deep understanding of the platform. Here are some effective strategies to organically grow your TikTok audience:

1. **Create High-Quality Content**: Quality content is the foundation of any organic growth strategy. Ensure your videos are well-produced, entertaining, informative, or creative depending on your niche. The more engaging your content is, the more likely users will follow you.

2. **Post Regularly**: Consistency is key on TikTok. Establish a regular posting schedule, whether it's once a day, several times a week, or whatever frequency fits your schedule. Followers appreciate consistency.

3. **Use Hashtags Strategically**: As mentioned earlier, hashtags are essential for your content's visibility. Use them wisely by selecting relevant hashtags for your niche and keeping an eye on popular trends.

4. **Be Active and Engage**: Respond to comments on your videos, interact with other creators, and stay active on the platform. The more you engage with the community, the more attention you'll draw to your account.

5. **Collaborate with Other Creators**: Collaborating with other creators can help you reach new audiences. Look for creators whose content complements yours and propose collaborations.

6. **Use Live Streams**: Live streams are a great way to create real-time interactions with your audience. Host Q&A sessions, live challenges, or discussions on topics relevant to your niche.

7. **Jump on Trends**: If a popular trend on TikTok is relevant to your content, take advantage of it. Create your version of the trend to attract attention from users following it.

8. **Analyze Your Metrics**: Use TikTok's analytics tools to understand what works and what doesn't on your account. Identify your best-performing videos and learn from them to shape your future strategy.

9. **Be Authentic**: Stay true to your personality and style. Users are drawn to authenticity, so be yourself in your videos.

10. **Share on Other Platforms**: If you have other social media accounts, share your TikTok videos on these platforms to draw in an already engaged audience.

11. **Include Calls to Action**: Encourage viewers to follow, like, comment, or share your content by including calls to action in your videos.

12. **Stay Up to Date**: Follow current TikTok trends and adapt your content accordingly. Stay flexible and open to changes in the algorithm and audience preferences.

Growing your audience organically on TikTok takes time, but by consistently applying these strategies and staying engaged with your audience, you can gradually expand your follower base. Be patient, adapt your approach based on results, and keep creating high-quality content to succeed on TikTok.

Cross-Promotion on Other Social Platforms

Cross-promoting on other social platforms is a powerful strategy to boost your TikTok audience. Here's how to use this method effectively:

1. **Identify Your Other Platforms**: First, identify the other social platforms where you are active. This can include Instagram, Facebook, Twitter, YouTube, Snapchat, and other relevant social networks.

2. **Share Clips of Your TikTok Videos**: Use your other social accounts to share clips from your TikTok videos. Choose the most captivating moments to entice followers from other platforms to check out your TikTok profile.

3. **Add Links**: When sharing clips from your TikTok videos on other platforms, be sure to include a direct link to your TikTok profile in the description or bio of your other social accounts. This makes it easier for followers to move between platforms.

4. **Announce Your TikTok Videos**: Use your other social accounts to announce in advance

when you'll post new TikTok videos. This can create anticipation and encourage your followers to check out your TikTok profile at the time of publication.

5. **Use Stories or Status Features**: Use the Stories or Status features on other platforms to share previews of your TikTok videos. You can also include direct links to your TikTok videos for easy access.

6. **Share Highlights**: If one of your TikTok videos gets a lot of engagement or goes viral, share that highlight on your other social platforms. This can spark the interest of new followers who want to see more of your TikTok content.

7. **Engage Your Audience**: Encourage your followers on other platforms to interact with your TikTok content by asking questions, conducting polls, or seeking their feedback on your videos. The more involved they feel, the more likely they are to follow your TikTok profile.

8. **Collaborate with Other Creators**: If you collaborate with other creators who have a presence on other social platforms, make sure to mutually promote each other's content across all platforms. This can significantly expand your audience.

9. **Use Hashtag Strategies**: When sharing clips of your TikTok videos on other platforms, use relevant hashtags to increase the visibility of your posts. Hashtags help users discover your content more easily.

10. **Analyze the Data**: Monitor the performance of your cross-promotion efforts to understand what works best on each platform. Adapt your strategy based on the results.

Cross-promotion on other social platforms can be an extremely effective way to attract new followers to TikTok. It allows you to leverage your existing audience on other networks and encourage those followers to discover your TikTok content. Be consistent in your cross-promotion efforts and adapt your strategy based on feedback to optimize your growth on TikTok.

Using TikTok Ads

Using TikTok ads is a paid strategy to accelerate your audience growth and become a successful influencer on the platform. Here's an overview of how you can leverage TikTok ads to promote your content and grow your profile:

1. **Types of TikTok Ads**: TikTok offers several ad formats to help promote your account and videos. The main types of ads include In-Feed Ads, Account Promotion Ads, Hashtag Challenge Ads, and TopView Ads. Each format has its advantages depending on your goals.

2. **Promote Your Videos**: In-Feed ads are short video ads that appear directly in users' main feed. You can use this format to promote your existing TikTok videos to a wider audience. Make sure the video you're promoting is attractive and engaging to maximize impact.

3. **Increase Your Visibility**: Account promotion ads are designed to increase the number of followers on your TikTok account. They appear in the "Suggested Accounts" section and encourage users to follow your account after seeing your ad. This is an excellent way to gain new followers quickly.

4. **Launch Challenges**: Hashtag Challenge ads are ideal if you want to launch a TikTok challenge. You create a unique challenge hashtag, promote it with an ad, and encourage users to participate. This can help create an engaged community around your content.

5. **Leverage TopView Ads**: TopView ads are the first videos users see when they open the TikTok app. This is a great opportunity to showcase your content or profile in a bold way. However, this format can be more expensive.

6. **Target Your Audience**: TikTok offers advanced targeting options to ensure your ads reach the audience you are most interested in. You can target by age, gender, location, interests, and other criteria.

7. **Budget and Bidding**: You can set a daily budget for your TikTok ads and use the bidding system to compete with other advertisers. It's important to carefully monitor your ad spending to get the best return on investment.

8. **Tracking and Analysis**: TikTok provides tracking and analytics tools to evaluate the performance of your ads. Use this data to

optimize your campaigns and adjust your strategy based on the results.

9. **Create Compelling Content**: When creating TikTok ads, ensure your content is impactful, engaging, and aligned with TikTok's quality standards. A memorable ad can encourage users to explore your profile further.

10. **Be Strategic**: TikTok ads are an investment, so make sure you have a clear strategy in place. Consider your goals, target audience, and how ads fit into your overall TikTok strategy.

Using TikTok ads can be an effective way to promote your account, gain visibility, and quickly attract new followers. However, it's important to remember that quality content is still essential. Ads can help you grab attention, but it's your organic content that will keep and grow your audience. By wisely combining ads with quality content, you can increase your chances of becoming a successful influencer on TikTok.

Audience Data Analysis

Audience data analysis is a crucial step in becoming a successful influencer on TikTok. It allows you to understand who your followers are, how they interact with your content, and how you can improve your strategy to meet their expectations. Here's how to approach audience data analysis on TikTok effectively:

1. **Use TikTok Analytics Tools**: TikTok offers built-in analytics tools available through your business or creator account. These tools provide insights into your video performance, audience demographics, and audience engagement.

2. **Understand Your Audience**: Explore the demographic data of your audience, such as age, gender, location, and interests. Understand who makes up your audience and tailor your content accordingly.

3. **Analyze Video Performance**: Review individual statistics for each video you've posted. Look at the number of views, likes, comments, and shares. Identify which videos

performed best and look for trends in those videos.

4. **Identify Trends and Popular Topics**: Audience data can show you which topics and types of content are most popular with your audience. Use this information to guide your future content creation.

5. **Evaluate Engagement**: Audience engagement is a key indicator of the quality of your content. Analyze engagement rates, such as the interaction rate (likes, comments, shares) compared to the number of views. The higher the engagement, the more your content resonates with your audience.

6. **Monitor Audience Growth**: Track your follower growth over time. Identify periods when you gained or lost a significant number of followers and try to understand what contributed to these fluctuations.

7. **Identify Optimal Posting Times**: Audience statistics can indicate when your followers are most active during the day. Use this information to schedule your posts at times that maximize your content's visibility.

8. **Test New Strategies**: Use audience data to guide your experiments. For example, if you

notice tutorial-style videos are popular, try creating more content in that style.

9. **Respond to Comments and Feedback**: Your audience's comments are valuable. Read and respond to them. Audience feedback can help you improve your content and build a stronger relationship with your followers.

10. **Stay Flexible**: Audience data evolves over time, just like your followers' preferences. Stay flexible and ready to adjust your strategy based on new insights you receive.

Analyzing audience data on TikTok is an ongoing process that allows you to optimize your content strategy to attract and retain a larger audience. By understanding who your followers are, what they like, and how they interact with your content, you can make informed decisions to improve your presence on the platform and become a successful influencer. Remember that data analysis should be combined with an authentic and creative approach to maximize your success on TikTok.

Chapter 6

Monetization and Personal Brand Management

Different Ways to Earn Money on TikTok (Sponsorships, Merch, Ads)

Monetization on TikTok has become a reality for many influencers. In this chapter, we'll explore different ways to earn money on TikTok, including sponsorships, merchandise, and advertisements.

1. **Sponsorships:**
   Sponsorships are one of the most common methods for influencers to earn money on TikTok. Here's how it works:
   • **Brand Collaborations:** You can collaborate with brands interested in your audience and content. These brands will pay you to promote their products or services in your videos.
   • **Discount Codes and Affiliate Links:** You can also get a discount code or affiliate link to promote the brand's products. Every time someone uses your code or link to make a purchase, you earn a commission.

2. **Merchandise:**

   Creating merchandise can be a source of income for influencers with a loyal fan base. Here are some merchandise ideas you can sell:

   • **Merch:** You can sell items like t-shirts, hats, stickers, and other personalized products with your logo or quotes from your videos.

   • **Online Courses or Training:** If you have expertise in a particular field, you can create paid online courses or training sessions for your interested followers.

3. **Advertisements:**

   Advertising is another potential revenue source on TikTok. Here's how it can work:

   • **TikTok Monetization Program:** TikTok offers a monetization program where eligible creators can earn money from their videos. This includes ad revenue sharing and virtual gifts from viewers.

   • **Branded Ads:** Brands may pay you to create and share ad videos for their products or services on your TikTok account.

4. **Affiliate   Offers:**

   Some companies offer affiliate programs where you can promote their products or services in exchange for a commission on sales generated by your recommendations.

5. **Live Stream Gifts:** When you go live on TikTok, viewers can send you virtual gifts using virtual currency. You can then convert these gifts into real money.

6. **Selling Original Music:** If you create original music for your TikTok videos, you can sell it on streaming platforms like iTunes, Spotify, or Apple Music.

7. **Personal Brand Management:** In addition to monetization, managing your personal brand is essential to maintaining your success on TikTok. Here are some tips:
   • **Stay Consistent:** Ensure that your content remains consistent with your niche and personality. Your followers need to know what to expect.
   • **Be Transparent:** If you're doing advertisements or sponsorships, be transparent with your audience. Honesty is crucial to maintaining trust with your followers.
   • **Engage with Your Audience:** Respond to comments, host Q&A sessions, and build an authentic connection with your audience.
   • **Avoid Burnout:** The constant pressure to create content can lead to burnout. Take care of your mental health and take breaks when needed.

• **Diversify Your Income Streams:** Don't rely on just one income source. Diversify your activities to reduce financial risks. Monetization and personal brand management on TikTok can be an exciting journey for influencers. However, it's essential to stay true to your style and authenticity throughout the process. Build your reputation as a trusted creator on the platform, and your monetization opportunities will grow over time.

Building a Strong Personal Brand

Building a strong personal brand is key to becoming a successful influencer on TikTok. Your personal brand encompasses your identity, style, values, and how people perceive you. Here's how to build a strong personal brand on TikTok:

1. **Identify Your Niche:**
   The first step to building a strong personal brand is defining your niche. What are you passionate about, and what do you want to explore on TikTok? Identify this area and focus on creating content related to it.

2. **Be Authentic:**
   Authenticity is key to establishing a connection with your audience. Be yourself in your videos, sharing your opinions, experiences, and personality genuinely. TikTok users appreciate truthfulness and transparency.

3. **Create a Recognizable Style:**
   Develop a content creation style that's uniquely yours. This could include the way you speak, the types of effects you use, or

even your clothing style. A consistent style will help people recognize you instantly.

4. **Define Your Values:**
   Identify the values important to you and reflect them in your content. Your audience is more likely to connect with you if your values resonate with theirs.

5. **Create an Impactful Bio:**
   Your TikTok bio is where you make a strong first impression. Write a concise and catchy bio that summarizes your personality and content. Don't forget to include relevant keywords to help people find you.

6. **Be Consistent with Posting:**
   Consistency is crucial to maintaining audience engagement. Establish a regular posting schedule so your followers know when to expect new content.

7. **Use Relevant Hashtags:**
   Use hashtags relevant to your niche to increase the visibility of your videos. Look for trends and popular hashtags in your field.

8. **Engage with Your Audience:**
   Respond to comments, ask questions, and encourage interaction with your audience. Create a community around your content.

9. **Collaborate with Other Creators:**
   Collaborating with other creators can help you expand your audience and strengthen your personal brand. Choose creators whose content complements yours.

10. **Evolve with Your Audience:**
    Your audience will evolve over time. Take note of comments and feedback to adjust your content and stay relevant.

11. **Educate and Entertain:**
    Offer a balanced mix of education and entertainment in your content to attract different types of viewers.

12. **Be Patient:**
    Building a strong personal brand takes time. Don't expect immediate results. Stay persistent and keep creating quality content. Building a strong personal brand on TikTok takes time and effort, but it can lead to significant opportunities for collaboration, monetization, and growth. When you have a well-established personal brand, viewers are more likely to follow and engage with your content. Remember, the key is to stay authentic and create content that resonates with your target audience.

Managing Brand Relationships and Partnerships

Managing brand relationships and partnerships is a vital skill for TikTok influencers. These partnerships can be an essential source of income and growth opportunities, but they must be managed professionally and strategically. Here's how to effectively manage brand relationships and partnerships on TikTok:

1. **Identify the Right Brands:**

   Choose brands that align with your niche and values. Working with brands that fit your content and audience is essential to maintaining the consistency of your personal brand.

2. **Establish Selection Criteria:**

   Before accepting a partnership, set clear criteria for evaluating brands. Consider factors such as the brand's reputation, the relevance of their products or services, the payment offered, and content expectations.

3. **Be Transparent:**

When collaborating with a brand, be transparent with your audience. Clearly mention that the video is sponsored or part of a paid partnership. Honesty strengthens trust with your audience.

4. **Negotiate Partnership Terms:**

Discuss the details of the partnership with the brand, including the expected content, posting period, payment, image usage rights, and any other important aspects. Ensure both sides understand the expectations.

5. **Create High-Quality Content:**

When creating content for a partnership, ensure it's high quality and aligns with your usual style. Sponsored videos should be authentic and engaging.

6. **Meet Deadlines:**

Stick to the deadlines agreed upon with the brand. Punctuality is crucial for maintaining a good reputation with brands.

7. **Communicate Professionally:**

Ensure that your communication with brands is professional and polite. Be responsive to emails and messages to maintain a good working relationship.

8. **Protect Your Rights:**

Before publishing sponsored content, clarify the rights to the video. Determine if the brand can reuse the content on its own platforms or in other advertising campaigns.

9. **Evaluate Results:**

After publishing the sponsored video, monitor its performance. Review the video's statistics to assess the partnership's impact. Was it beneficial for both the brand and yourself?

10. **Preserve Your Credibility:**

Choose partnerships wisely to avoid overloading your TikTok account with sponsored content. Too many collaborations can harm your credibility and audience engagement.

11. **Be Ready to Negotiate:**

In some cases, it may be necessary to negotiate the partnership terms, including payment. Be prepared to advocate for the value of your audience and content.

12. **Provide Constructive Feedback:**

Once the partnership is over, share constructive feedback with the brand. This can help establish long-term relationships and improve future partnerships.

Effectively managing brand relationships and partnerships on TikTok requires balancing authentic content creation with the brand's goals. By focusing on transparency, content quality, and professionalism, you can build fruitful partnerships and maintain a strong reputation as a TikTok influencer.

Chapter 7
Ethics and Responsibility as an Influencer

Responsibility as an Influencer

Responsibility as an influencer on TikTok is a crucial aspect of your journey as a content creator. As someone who impacts an audience, you have a responsibility to exercise your influence ethically and thoughtfully. Here's how to approach responsibility as an influencer on TikTok:

1. **Impact on the Audience:** Understand that your content can have an impact on your followers, especially if they are young or impressionable. Be aware of the potential impact of your words and actions.

2. **Authenticity:** Stay authentic in your content. Do not promote products or opinions you don't genuinely believe in, as this can compromise your credibility with your audience.

3. **Transparency:** Be transparent about sponsored partnerships and advertisements. Clearly mention when your content is sponsored to maintain your audience's trust.

4. **Moderation:** Use moderation in your videos and comments to promote a respectful environment. Remove or block offensive or inappropriate comments.

5. **Promotion of Positive Values:** Use your influence to promote positive values such as tolerance, inclusion, diversity, and respect. Avoid spreading hateful or discriminatory messages.

6. **Caution Regarding Health and Wellness:** If discussing topics related to physical or mental health, ensure that you provide accurate and responsible information. Avoid giving medical advice without professional expertise.

7. **Online Safety:** Raise awareness among your audience about online safety risks such as harassment, cyberbullying, and scams. Encourage safe online behaviors.

8. **Education and Continuous Learning:** Be willing to learn and evolve. Stay informed about trends, emerging ethical issues, and best practices in content creation.

9. **Responsible Engagement:** When interacting with your audience, demonstrate respect and empathy. Avoid promoting dangerous or destructive behaviors.

10. **Prevention of Deviations:** Be aware of signs of potential deviations in your content or behavior. If you identify issues, take steps to correct them promptly.

11. **Respect for Platform Rules:** Adhere to TikTok's content, advertising, and copyright rules. Avoid violating platform guidelines.

12. **Responsibility to Partners:** If you have partnerships with brands, honor the terms of the contract and provide the agreed-upon content on time.

As an influencer on TikTok, you have a powerful platform to communicate with the world, and with this power comes great responsibility. Your audience relies on you to provide quality, ethical, and respectful content. By maintaining high standards of responsibility and ethics, you can not only build a strong reputation but also positively contribute to the TikTok community and society at large. Responsibility as an influencer is not just an obligation; it's an opportunity to make a positive impact on others' lives.

Issues of Safety and Privacy

Safety and privacy issues are major concerns for TikTok influencers, given the public and viral nature of the platform. It's essential to understand these issues and take steps to protect your own safety and that of your audience. Here's how to address these concerns:

1. **Personal Security:**

   o **Protect Your Personal Information:** Do not share sensitive personal information such as your address, phone number, or bank details on TikTok. The information you share online can be used against you.

   o **Manage Your Geolocation:** Be cautious about using geolocation in your videos. Avoid sharing information about your current location in real time, which could compromise your safety.

   o **Use Strong Passwords:** Ensure that your TikTok account is secured with a strong, unique password. Enable two-factor authentication if possible.

- o **Limit Access to Your Accounts:** Do not share your account credentials with others, and ensure that you are the only person accessing your account.

2. **Respect for Privacy:**

- o **Obtain Consent:** If you include others in your videos, make sure to get their consent for recording and publishing. Respect the privacy of others.

- o **Be Cautious with Others' Personal Information:** Avoid disclosing or sharing personal information belonging to others, even if they appear in your videos.

3. **Managing Comments and Interactions:**

- o **Monitor Comments:** Regularly monitor the comments on your videos. Remove offensive comments, harassment, or inappropriate content.

- o **Block Harmful Users:** If you receive comments or messages from harmful individuals, block them to prevent access to your content.

4. **Awareness of Cyberbullying:**

   o **Educate Your Audience:** Raise awareness among your audience about cyberbullying and encourage a positive online environment. Urge your followers to report any bullying behavior.

   o **Take Action in Case of Cyberbullying:** If you are a victim of cyberbullying, report the behavior to the platform and take steps to protect your own mental and emotional well-being.

5. **Financial Security:**

   o **Beware of Scams:** Be vigilant regarding suspicious offers or proposals. Do not share financial or personal information with strangers claiming to provide lucrative opportunities.

   o **Protect Your Bank Account:** If you are compensated by partnerships or collaborations, ensure that transactions are secure and legitimate. Use reputable payment platforms.

Safety and privacy are crucial aspects of managing your presence on TikTok. By taking measures to protect your own safety and that of your audience, you can create a positive and secure online environment. Also, ensure to inform your audience about good practices regarding safety and privacy, helping to raise awareness and protect TikTok users.

Using Your Influence Positively

Using your influence positively is one of the most important responsibilities as an influencer on TikTok. Your ability to influence your audience's opinions and behaviors gives you a unique opportunity to make a positive difference in the world. Here's how you can maximize the positive impact of your influence on TikTok:

1. **Educate and Inform:** Use your platform to educate your audience on important topics. Whether it's factual information, practical advice, or raising awareness on social issues, your content can be a valuable source of knowledge.

2. **Raise Awareness for Important Causes:** Identify causes or social issues that matter to you and use your voice to raise awareness among your audience. Encourage support for charities or awareness campaigns.

3. **Promote Tolerance and Inclusion:** Advocate for tolerance, inclusion, and respect for diversity. Use your influence to fight against

discrimination, racism, homophobia, and other forms of prejudice.

4. **Inspire and Motivate:** Share inspiring stories, personal development challenges, and advice to help your followers improve their lives. Serve as inspiration by sharing your own growth and success experiences.

5. **Provide Emotional Support:** Recognize that your followers may face personal challenges. Offer emotional support by encouraging discussion or sharing resources on mental health and well-being.

6. **Promote Positive Behaviors:** Encourage positive behaviors such as altruism, kindness, environmental respect, and social responsibility.

7. **Avoid Spreading Misinformation:** Be diligent in verifying the information you share. Do not spread misinformation, fake news, or conspiracy theories.

8. **Take Responsibility for Your Actions:** Be aware of the potential impact of your words and actions. Ensure that your content adheres to high ethical standards.

9. **Collaborate for Change:** Collaborate with other influencers, charities, or advocacy

groups for projects aimed at bringing about positive changes in society.

10. **Listen to Your Audience:** Pay attention to your audience's concerns, feedback, and needs. Consider their opinions to guide your content toward topics that matter to them.

11. **Be a Positive Role Model:** Serve as a positive role model by demonstrating exemplary behaviors and attitudes in your videos and personal life.

The positive influence you can exert as a TikTok influencer should not be underestimated. You have the opportunity to inspire, inform, and mobilize thousands, if not millions, through your content. This entails a moral and ethical responsibility to do good with your influence, contribute to a better world, and set an example for your audience. By using your influence positively, you can create a lasting and meaningful impact in the lives of others.

Chapter 8

The Evolution of TikTok and Future Trends

The Latest Developments in TikTok

TikTok is a dynamic platform that is constantly evolving to meet the changing needs of its user community. In this chapter, we will explore the latest developments on TikTok and anticipate the future trends that could shape the platform's landscape.

The Latest Developments in TikTok:

1. **Algorithms and Content Discovery:** TikTok continues to enhance its algorithms to further personalize the content appearing in users' feeds. This includes a better understanding of user preferences and highlighting relevant videos.

2. **Monetization for Creators:** TikTok has introduced new monetization features for creators, including the TikTok Creator Fund and the ability to receive donations from fans. These options enable influencers to earn money directly on the platform.

3. **Special Effects and Content Creation:** TikTok has continued to expand its library of special effects and creation tools to allow users to create even more original and creative videos.

4. **Live Streaming:** Live broadcasts on TikTok have become increasingly popular, allowing creators to interact with their audience in real-time and receive virtual gifts in return.

5. **E-commerce:** TikTok has experimented with integrated e-commerce features, allowing users to make purchases directly from the platform. Influencers can also promote products in their videos.

Future Trends for TikTok:

1. **Content Diversification:** TikTok is expected to continue diversifying the types of supported content. New categories such as education, politics, and health could gain importance.

2. **Virtual Creation Spaces:** Virtual reality (VR) and augmented reality (AR) could play an increasingly important role on TikTok, offering users new immersive experiences.

3. **Strengthening Monetization:** TikTok is likely to continue developing monetization

options for creators, paving the way for new revenue opportunities.

4. **Security and Privacy Protection:** TikTok will probably continue to strengthen security and privacy measures to protect its users, especially younger ones.

5. **Cultural and Social Trends:** TikTok is often at the forefront of cultural and social trends. The platform will continue to be a place where new trends in dance, music, fashion, and behavior emerge.

6. **Partnerships with Celebrities:** Partnerships with celebrities and brands are expected to continue, enhancing TikTok's visibility and opening new opportunities for creators.

7. **International Development:** TikTok will continue to expand into new international markets, which could lead to the emergence of new influencers and trends specific to those regions.

It is essential for aspiring TikTok influencers to stay updated with the platform's developments and adapt to emerging trends. By understanding the latest features and anticipating future trends, creators can maximize their success on TikTok and continue to build their audience. The key is to remain creative, engaged, and responsive to the needs of your community and the platform's evolution.

Predictions and Future Trends

By anticipating future trends on TikTok, aspiring influencers can prepare to remain relevant and maximize their success on the platform. While the future is always uncertain, here are some potential predictions and trends that could shape the TikTok landscape in the coming years:

1. **Content Diversification:** TikTok will likely continue to diversify the types of supported content. Creators may explore new niches and content categories, moving beyond dance and comedy videos to address topics such as education, politics, mental health, cooking, and more.

2. **Evolution of Formats:** Content formats will evolve. Interactive videos, multi-part series, and augmented or virtual reality videos could become more common. Challenges and dance trends will remain significant, but other formats will gain popularity.

3. **Expanding Monetization:** TikTok will continue to develop monetization options for creators. Influencers will have more

opportunities to earn money through sponsored partnerships, affiliations, product sales, and fan gifts.

4. **Security and Privacy Protection:** The platform will continue to enhance security measures to protect its users, especially younger ones. Parental controls and safety tools will be improved.

5. **Social and Political Impact:** TikTok could become a more influential space for discussing social and political issues. Creators may use their platforms to raise awareness about important issues and mobilize their audience around causes.

6. **International Expansion:** TikTok will continue to expand into new international markets. This could lead to cultural diversification of content and the emergence of new influencers from different regions of the world.

7. **Cutting-Edge Technology:** Technological advancements, such as artificial intelligence, augmented reality, and virtual reality, could be integrated into content creation on TikTok, providing users with more immersive experiences.

8. **Limitless Creativity:** TikTok creators will continue to push the boundaries of creativity. Emerging trends may focus on visual creativity, innovative special effects, and engaging storytelling.

9. **Online Education:** TikTok could become a more serious learning platform. Creators could share knowledge and skills, offering mini-courses and tutorials in various fields.

10. **Mentorship Among Creators:** Established influencers could play a mentoring role for newcomers, sharing their advice and expertise to help other creators succeed on the platform.

11. **Cross-Platform Collaborations:** Collaborations between TikTok and other social media platforms could become more frequent, allowing creators to reach a wider audience.

It is important to note that TikTok is a constantly evolving platform, and trends can change rapidly. Content creators must remain flexible, creative, and attentive to the evolving preferences of their audience. By investing time in understanding the platform and following future developments, aspiring influencers can stay competitive and continue to build their success on TikTok.

Conclusion

Encouragement for Future Influencers

In this guide, we have explored in detail the key elements for becoming a successful influencer on TikTok. This exciting journey can be both rewarding and fulfilling, but it also requires dedication, creativity, and hard work. As a conclusion, here are some encouragements and tips for future TikTok influencers:

1. **Be Authentic:** Your authenticity is your most valuable asset as an influencer. Stay true to yourself, share your passions, and showcase your unique personality. Your audience will be drawn to your genuine nature.

2. **Persevere:** Success as an influencer doesn't happen overnight. It may take time to build a loyal audience and for your content to be noticed. Be patient and keep persevering.

3. **Learn Continuously:** The social media landscape is evolving rapidly. Stay informed about the latest trends, new TikTok features, and best content practices. Continuous learning is essential.

4. **Create Quality Content:** The quality of your content is crucial. Invest time in creating engaging, well-produced, and original videos. Always seek to improve.

5. **Build Relationships:** Establish authentic relationships with your audience. Engage with your followers by responding to their comments, asking questions, and listening to their feedback.

6. **Be Responsible:** Remember the responsibility that comes with influence. Use your voice ethically, respectfully, and responsibly. Be a positive role model for your audience.

7. **Experiment and Be Creative:** Don't be afraid to experiment with new types of content, video styles, and subjects. Creativity is one of the keys to success on TikTok.

8. **Don't Underestimate Your Audience:** Your followers may be diverse and have varied interests. Don't underestimate their ability to appreciate different types of content.

9. **Stay Updated:** Keep up with TikTok's evolution, stay informed about new features, and watch for emerging trends. This will help you remain competitive on the platform.

10. **Have Fun:** Finally, don't forget to enjoy yourself. The passion and enthusiasm you bring to your content are contagious. If you're having fun, it's likely that your audience will too.

Diving into the world of influence on TikTok can be an exciting journey, filled with opportunities to share your voice, talents, and passions with the world. So go for it, be persistent, and continue to create content that resonates with your audience. You have the potential to become a successful influencer on TikTok and make a positive impact in the social media community. Good luck!

www.ingramcontent.com/pod-product-compliance
Lightning Source LLC
LaVergne TN
LVHW051742050326
832903LV00029B/2665